Tetiana's Adventures in Wonderlaw

A fairy-tale about law and justice
and brief introduction to
the common law of the realm
for students from civil code countries

by

Dr.Jur. Eric Engle, LL.M.

DEDICATION

This book is for fairies, knights, and princesses who believe in
Justice through law.

CONTENTS

ACKNOWLEDGMENTS

For Tetiana Danyliuk

Presented to Tetiana Danyliuk in recognition of her achievement in gaining admission to the University of California, Berkeley, Law School as a sign of my admiration of her steadfast commitment to justice and her faith in the rule of law and intelligence.

Tetiana's Adventure in Wonderlaw

A GRIMM FORWARD:
LAWS MOULDERING EMPIRE

*Lawyers are inflexible, law is inflexible, and indeed
there is much to hate, loathe and revile in the law.
There is some beauty in the law but it is exceptional.
It is a mouldering dead yet beautiful world of love,
fear, hopes, desires, and – honestly - disappointments:*

The ruined glory of mighty minds.

*Out of these miscast minds sometimes sprout feeble flowers
of hope and love. But, these exceptions are found amidst
the choking weeds of lies and the rubble of failed dreams.
rubble of failed dreams.*

*The sky, clouded by treachery,
is lit only by the dark light of greed.
Such is laws empire, the abode of dead ideas.*

ideas.

1

CHAPTER ZERO:
THROUGH THE LOOKINGLASS

This part of our story is most sensible and useful
to people who know German law or the
laws of countries who use German laws such as Japan,
China, Russia, Greece and Eastern European
countries. If comparative law is not "your cup of tea",
dear reader, please simply skip this forword,

Similarities and Differences Between German and US Law

for ignorance is bliss, is it knot?

Most of US and German law is basically the same. Not all of it.

The most important difference is the law versus equity distinction, which does not exist in German

law. This is big. Note it. Law, Equity – different. Learn it!

Foreign lawyers must be careful to understand equity, for there is no equivalent in civil law

countries. That is also big, important:

Equity is an exceptional discretionary remedy offered by the court in the interest of justice as

a corrective of the law,

for examples, where the law did not foresee certain facts or was simply badly drafted.

3

Equity, or more exactly equitable remedies, are court crafted remedies. Equity is an exception to the common law adversarial system. In common law countries, the judge is almost always merely a passive neutral observer, an arbiter of competing arguments. That is an adversarial, as opposed to an inquisitorial system. Equity is an intervention by the court into the operation of the law; one which the parties must ask for, true, but

once the litigants 0pen pandora's box

the judge is then free to bring out any of the equitable remedies the judge regards as fitting and just.

Law *is lex scripta: writings. Thus, contracts, legislation, constitutions, all are law, not equity.*

Equity can be recognized in that **any remedy other than money damages is an equitable remedy**.
At law you have only one remedy: money.
Of course there are things which matter more than money, but law and justice can only do so much.

One may not come into equity with unclean hands.
To obtain equity one must comply with the
equitable maxims. The principle maxims follow:
He who seeks equity must do equity.
Equity rewards the vigilant, not those who slumber on their rights.
Equity is equality.
Between equal equities, first in time prevails.
Equity follows the law.
Equity acts in personam.
Equity delights in justice, and not by halves.
For now just memorize these maxims.

Memorize them. I will explain them as they arise. I
generally recommend ***against*** memorizing. Lord
Justice Coke rightly said that you must understand
the principles and purposes of the law rather than
individual rules or decisions, and he is right, with
one exception. Memorizing the equitable principles
and the various equitable remedies will help
you immensely because equity is lex non scripta – unwritten law.
Other important differences between
common law and law in countries with a civil code:
The doctrine of **consideration** in contract law (infra).

The **tenurial system**
of land ownership,
a leftover from feudalism
wherein knights
would possess

land

in *exchange*
for military service,

is also alien

to civil law systems..

6

And thus, the various names of interests in land in common law countries are also different from the civil law countries.

The most important possessory interests in land are:
Fee simple absolute
Fee simple subject to condition subsequent
Remainders
Reversions
Life estates
Estates for a term of years
Tenancy by the entireties
Joint tenants with right of survivorship
Tenancy in common

Easements, covenants, encumbrances,and servitudes

equitable or legal are also important interests in land which are however non-possessory.

You will need to learn all these terms for the bar exam.
Easements
and
Equitable servitudes
are very similar: an easement is a property interest at law, an equitable servitude is an interest recognized, if at all, in equity.

These are also tested on the bar exam.

Adverse possession / acquisition of title by prescription.

Some rules of evidence also do not exist in civil law countries:
The rule against perpetuities
The parole evidence rule
The statute of frauds
The rule against hearsay (and all its exceptions)

are all rules
our heroine
must learn
in order
to pass her
bar exam!

7   *SHE SHALL PASS!*

So:
equity
and
evidence
are different from German or French civil-code law systems.

Contract law is mostly like German or French law. However, the *parole evidence rule,* the *statute of frauds,* and the doctrine of *consideration* in contracts are unique to countries which use the common law of England. Finally, there are no joking declarations of intent (Scherzerklärung). In common law - you joke at your own peril! ! !

Jest, but Lightly!

German and U.S. Constitutional law
are just about exactly the same.

This surprised me, but nevertheless it is true.

One exception: advisory opinions are prohibited in
U.S. law but are part of German law. Also there
is no third party effect of constitutional law on
private litigants relations inter-se in U.S. law. .

Torts - similar
European and American Administrative law
are very similar and is not on the bar.

Tax - very similar

So, this briefest of introductories allows us
to move into studying the common law.

9

CHAPTER ONE:
A GIRL, IN LOVE

Once upon a time there was a **beautiful** young *intelligent* Girl.
Omg! :D

                           And though she did not
know it,

       she was a princess!

This girl was full of *faith* and *hope* and *love*.

And this particular girl had a particular belief:
    she
           believed
   in
                    justice!

She knew how to divide pi *fairly.*

And, what makes this silly girl quite interesting, is this.

she actually believed that the best way to

attain justice was through law!

O, how naive!

The writ of the Princess equitable:

"Three points:
One for all!"

Now to the table!

Enjoy your pi!

Yet she persisted in her belief, stubbornly, for that
was the kind of princess she is, although she does
not know it. So, being called naive at times she
went to seek solace for injustice in law's desolate

landscape. She searched through towers of books and walls of authority all in search of a fleeting glimpse of another girl, named
Justitia v.,
whom she loved very very much.

No. Even more than that!

And that is the love story, which is the topic of our little fairy tale.

PARAMOUNT OWNERSHIP

Now, the PARAMOUNT owner is she who hold best title.

So for example the QUEEN of

ENGLAND is PARAMOUNT to all other owners in her realm.

Likewise, the fee simple owner, a Knight, is paramount
 to the tenant, and the tenant is paramount to

their sublessor, and so it goes: the fairies of course are
the paramount owners of unicorns, who in

turn are paramount owners of silver bells, and cockle shells.
 Pretty maids in a row are however

15   *owned by no one!*

Thus for example you are paramount owner of a **watch**.

But, suppose you are lax and I am sly,
and I take your watch from you!

OMG. Now I know WHY he is in a rush and so very very late!

And I then run away, and throw it into a rabbit hole,
 so as not to be caught, secreting your watch so
that I may complete my theft thereof (for it is theft:
caption+asportation+animus furundi=theft).

16

I then recover
your watch, and
am now holding it!

For I,
a simple Rabbit
did indeed
learn from the
shrewd foxes,

in

peril

of

my

life!

I have taken and carried your watch away with
the intent to deprive. (this is advanced English
vocabulary, and English is properly spelled like that).
Yet, though I am the most wrongful holder possible,
so long as that watch is in my possession I am
presumed to have good title to it: and the law makes
me *responsible* for its treatment. The property
right being the right to use, to abuse, and to
profits from the property (usus, abusus, and
fructus=property) -- If I abuse that property, You
have a definite claim not only to that res, the thing,
but ALSO to the damages I inflicted; here my prayer,
may I never inflict damage, to another's property!

17

The true owner of property may use reasonable self-help to recover their property, however any use of force must be necessary and proportional. Throwing defenceless thieving bunny rabbits who steal watches into glass pantries is probably disproportional, rabbits have no fangs. Don't ask me what happens to Jaberwocky thieves, it is even uglier – they are armed with claws that catch and Jaws. Consequently, a greater use of force would be reasonable. However, while one may use deadly force where necessary in defence of one's own life one may not use deadly force in defence of property at common law.

YET suppose a wanderer, knowing not who owns the watch finds it! Now they are in good faith possession and have the rights to the watch against all the world save you, the true owner. Your remedy against them is REPLEVIN. You may replevy even from a good faith purchaser for value, if the court rule that such be in the interest of justice as an equitable remedy.

"By court order I replevy the watch! Now Give it back!"

The equitable remedy of replevin is a writ which shall issue
ordering delivery of possession (=livery of seisin) of the res
(=thing) to the true owner. Might you have damages for
abusus thereof? Yes! For it is not their bad faith, which is
punished, but your property interest which is compensated.
And thus though I, a common thief, am liable not only for
ordinary damages, but also for punitive damages, which are
offered by the court as justice requires (you may request
them- the court may or may not grant them), the good faith
finder can ONLY be liable for ordinary damages. Punitive
damages are a civil remedy for willful wanton and malicious
misconduct; there are penal remedies against the thief.
A writ is simply an order from the court,
ordering someone to do something.

That toilet looks awful uncomfortable, Mister Thief.

But suppose the good faith finder has read his bible, and does not "bury his talents" instead taking the watch, pawning it for money, to invest in the stock market, and makes money, buying low and selling high!
O frabjous day!

"How did you ever afford this lovely shop, you old granny goat?"
"Succesful speculation on the stock market: buy low, sell high!"

 Might you have the profits?

Yes! Certainly against the bad faith holder of your property.

Possibly not however against a good faith holder.

"Give me back my cane AND the money you made using it!
I replevy my cane back and

disgorge the wrongful profits!"

Your remedy would be equitable, specifically, to obtain your
expectancy interest you would institute an action before the court
of equity for EQUITABLE ACCOUNTING. Equitable accounting
awards realized profits to the rightful owner resulting from their
misappropriated property: Like any other equitable remedy,
equitable accounting is a court crafted remedy tailored to the
specific case at bar and is wholly discretionary! You do not have
a Right to equitable remedies but may seek them;
if the court finds your case compelling it may award them
but that is within the court's discretion

"Equity is a purely DISCRETIONARY remedy, hahahahah"
were the last words the Cheshire cat did not speak...

If the court awards the remedy of equitable accounting then I am forced to disgorge the profits I wrongly made. I must pay you back "in spades": I am liable for funds of yours which I spent on all those fine

But you might well NOT have the remedy of equitable accounting against the good faith finder. Yet, you certainly would have it against the common thief, presuming you are not in pari delicto. You may seek an equitable remedy only if you are equitable and acting in good faith:

equity rewards the vigilant, not those who slumber on their rights; she who seeks equity must do equity.

The inequitable OR imprudent have no remedy at equity!

The pawn broker has BAILED your property. The pawn brokerhas POSSESION but NOT Title, nor even a presumption of title, unlike the usual case where possession implies good title. One of them is BAILOR the other BAILEE.

If my English is proper, the BAILOR BAILS their PROPERTY with the BAILEE who holds it as on deposit. The term bail is also used to indicate the money deposited with a court to secure the freedom of a prisoner pending their trial.

Now suppose however that the pawn broker's contract states that after a month without REDEMPTION (for we REDEEM deposits) that title shall pass to him. And Mister Finder has not redeemed. Now imagine that the broker sells YOUR watch, to Mister Byer. You may clearly replevin your watch from Mister Byer. May you seek damages? Presuming there was no injury to the property, no. The buyer enjoys the usual presumption, that everyone acts in good faith, and thus there is no liability for damages beyond the value of the property itself. But may Byer seek damages against Pawn? Likely not, for they took on the risk that the property was stolen. Recall that Byer will have the burden of proof in his claim against Pawn, and that decides it here, since the moving party bears the burden of proof, and since Pawn did not act in bad faith, Byer cannot obtain damages.

25

However, had Pawn sold the watch PRIOR to the contractual date of 1 month for redemption, then Byer clearly would have damages AND be able to replevy the watch back from whoever has it regardless of their good faith in purchasing the stolen object.

Suppose instead that Pawn holds YOUR watch, and his brokerage is destroyed in a fire, which is covered by insurance. The fire destroys the watch, for gold melts at a fairly low temperature, and the chaos and destruction prevent finding the lost melted gold, which may be in the dirt or have been removed by a fireman or looter.

The accused thief shall have a jury of his peers
who will pass judgement on him...

However, while the common law will give you punitive damages against the thief, to toss the thief into prison requires an act of the public prosecutor.

All those dreams of riches – up in smoke – how sad!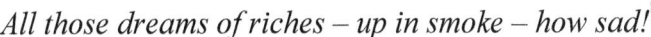

What then?

Mister Finder may obtain damages against Pawn, at least for breach of contract. You, too, may obtain damages against Pawn! For your property has been CONVERTED. You would as true owner have rights against Mister Finder.

Note however that as gold does not depreciate and is personal property there would be no lost interest as to the value of the item, a fortiori since such would be most likely de minimis. Interest on a 300 dollar watch for just one month is at most a few dollars, if that.

CHAPTER: CONTRACTS AND CONSIDERATION

"Curiouser and Curiouser, cried Tetiana!"

the rules in contract
law in German and
U.S. law are very
similar. One big
difference is the
doctrine of
consideration,
which does
not exist
in German law.
Consideration?
What is this
strange rule,
which does not exist
in German or French
civil law?
Suppose the Red Queen
makes a promise with
you as follows:
*"In consideration of
the attention you pay to me,
I promise to provide you wonderful instruction as to the laws
of the Red Queen."* And you accept the deal.
Is this promise enforceable?

The terms of a contract must be reasonably definite and certain.
Where a term is uncertain, the law may imply terms to a contract
which reflect the intention of the parties at the time of contracting.
So in terms of the terms of the above contract the law might imply
"a reasonable amount of instruction etc.".

But the issue here is, whether there is CONSIDERATION for the
promise. There is: each party gives something up and each party
gets something. They are in a "mutuality of obligation" which is

28

one way to define consideration.

To be a legally enforceable promise, the common law requires that there be "consideration", which is also known "bargained for exchange". There must be some exchange of values, whether in the form of actions or things or even renunications, if the promise is to be legally enforceable.

Perhaps the easiest way to understand consideration is to compare it to terms in German law: one might rightly translate consideration as "Wertaustausch" or "Gegenleistung". In French, as "contrepartie".

As far as legal concepts go, the legal concept of *causa*, in French also known as objet (du contrat) is the closest homologous legal concept. It may help to think that every contract in common law countries requires causa to be enforceable.

An "empty promise" is one unsupported by consideration.

Such a promise in common law is not enforceable as a contract, though it might be given some legal effect through the doctrine of estoppel or as evidence of a quasi contract.

Consideration thus requires an exchange of values, whether in the form of goods or services or even forebearances.

I must give something and get something just as you must give something and get something, in order for the contract to be enforceable.

An easy example might be where I sell you my book for a trumpet.
You give me the trumpet,
and I must then give you the **book**.
You obtain a book, I obtain a trumpet.

Here is your book,
take it from my hand!

There is clearly consideration
for that contract.

Once we understand consideration is merely the idea of an
exchange of values of some form or other other rules of
consideration follow: Consideration does not have to be
objectively equivalent values. The subjective value each party
places on their promise or performance is all that matters, not
the objective value. The law does not inquire into the adequacy
of consideration. I may sell you my house for merely one
dollar, and such consideration is adequate. Consideration may
be merely nominal, but must exist and may not be a mere
recital with no actual exchange: consideration cannot be
illusory. The next question is what may be consideration? May
it be goods? Of course. Services? Yes, they too may be
consideration. But what about forebearances, decisions not to
do something? These, too, may be consideration! What is
exchanged is broadly defined but something must be given up
by both parties for the bargain to be legally enforceable.
So for example in a famous case an uncle promised to give his
nephew a large amount of money for his birthday if the nephew
would not smoke.

The nephew agreed, and did not smoke.
Is this promise enforceable?
The court decided:

It was, because the nephew had undergone a detriment:
he had given up a legal right.

In a similar case, a hatter promised to use best-efforts to market
the wares of Lady Duff-Gordon.

This too was found to be adequate consideration.
The hatter obtained the exclusive use of Lady Duff Gordon's
famous name, and Lady Duff Gordon obtained (or ought to have
obtained) at least reasonable efforts from the hatter to market
the wares for commission.

So: **consideration may be** in the form of **a
benefit or a detriment, an action or forebearance.**

In contrast: **past consideration is no consideration**.
So if you state "in consideration of the tutoring
you have already received here is 10 dollars":
I cannot enforce that promise, at law.

*Past consideration is no consideration.
*Consideration may be nominal but must be real, not merely fictive.
*Consideration may be a benefit, detriment, action or forebearance
*Consideration may not be illusory. It must be real,
though it may be nominal.
*The law will not inquire into the adequacy of consideration:
that is for the parties to decide,
due to the principle of freedom of contract.

This is a jabberwocky. They are VERY dangerous.

Suppose the following statement by Knight:
*"I promise to slay the magical Jaberwocky
for 10 dollars and you may have its hide!"*

33

You agree. It is no enforcible contract. The consideration here, the slaying of the Jaberwocky and transfer of its hide, is illusory, since Jaberwocky's do not exist.

Suppose the following statement:

"In consideration of past services renderd,
I promise to pay you ten dollars." You agree.

This too is no enforceable promise, for the consideration has already been rendered.

I write you a letter. It says: "I will sell you my house for one dollar. I am serious!" and sign the letter. You then send me a letter with one dollar saying "I gladly accept your offer!" This **acceptance is effective on posting**, because of the mailbox rule, which creates a conclusive i.e. irrebuttable presumption of receipt of a letter properly posted at the time the letter is posted.

Is this an enforceable contract?

Acceptance is effective on posting, regardless of receipt,
and is irrevocable once posted.

I am sorry Mr. Walrus, you cannot have your letter back!

The consideration is adequate the acceptance valid. So, you buy my house, for just a dollar, and soon find out why it is so cheap: *it is a doll's house.*

Is our agreement an enfor  subjectively believed that I was selling a real house, when in fact I was selling a doll's house. If the objective facts make clear that with but reasonable inquiry you would have known that the house was but a doll's house the contract would stand. In contrast, if I were deceptive in any way or concealed the fact it was but a doll's house then the court would of course set aside the contract. Like in German law, the contract can be formed based on objective *or subjective agreement.* Thus if you said "bike" and we both knew we meant a bicycle, not a motorcycle, the contract would form, even though the word "bike" is a bit ambiguous.

So: regarding the house for a dollar. You, the buyer, may enforce the promise. The consideration, though nominal, is real, and **the law does not inquire into the adequacy of consideration**, only whether it exists.

Forebearances are decisions not to act in a way one might otherwise lawfully act. Forebearances can be consideration.
Here is the controverted case: you promise not to sue me in good faith, on a claim which is legally wrong; I pay $1000 to settle. Is it enforceable?
So long as the claim is in good faith, the forebearance of a legal right can be consideration. Such a promise is enforceable; the law encourages voluntary dispute settlement to avert costly litigation. The rule that the renunciation of a good faith legal claim, which is wrong on the law, can be valid consideration is such because claims are often controverted and uncertain.
May consideration be a performance, i.e. an action?
Yes, of course. For example: I promise to paint your house,

if you promise to pay me 1000 dollars on completion. You agree.
Is there a contract? There is a contract. This is a "promise
for a promise"

Early cases tried to distinguish promises from performances,
actions from forebearances, and also tried to figure out whether
it was the bargain or exchange which mattered. The current
doctrine of consideration is really well settled on all these issues!
Law school runs students through all the early cases in order to
teach students how the common law grows and also to teach legal
reasoning. I think that approach is mistaken, since these rules are
really well settled and can be exposited more rapidly, allowing
students to then focus on the currently unsettled or uncertain
areas of law.

Consideration is the idea that for a promise to be enforceable there
must be a bargained for exchange of values, whether as benefits
or detriments, actions or renunciation of actions. The closest
thing to consideration in German law is causa, which in French
is known as objet. These are similar, yet not exactly the same.
The best translations of consideration are "Gegenleistung",
"Contrepartie", possibly also "causa".

**Equitable remedies are also very different
and do not exist in the civil law countries.**
U.S. contract law is just about exactly like German law
But
since there is no civil code
there is less certainty
and more room for you to credibly argue for whatever you think
the law to be!

DAMAGES

The rules on damages, except for possible ***punitive damages***
in common law, are very similar to civil law countries. Punitive
damages are not recognized in civil law countries because they
are a penalty, and thus must meet the criminal standard of proof,
which is beyond reasonable doubt. In contrast, while British courts
normally award costs and fees to the winning party, the U.S.
courts generally do not, except in cases of abuse of process or
where punitive damages would be appropriate. In the civil law
countries of continental Europe the normal rule is the winner
takes all and the loser bears the price of the litigation for both
parties.

Otherwise however, the rules on **damages** are
are extremely similar in common law and civil law:1
Reliance damages are the negative Interesse:
costs incurred, payments made. They are easily
proven and thus not controverted, even as an equitable remedy.

The **expectancy damages** (positive Interesse also
 known as Erwartungsinteresse) **are the benefit
of the bargain**. To obtain these generally requires
an actual contract, though they may be reached
by the equitable remedy of quasi contract.
Pure economic losses (rein Vermögensschaden)
are generally not compensable in tort or even in
contract as they are too **speculative:**
they are also called **conseqeuential damages**
The rules on these types of damages are basically
the same both in common law and in civil law.
With respect to the measure of damages, the rules on damages
are just about exactly like in German civil law

LAND LAW

I sell you property, "To Tetiana and her heirs, so long as she uses it as a school. but if she uses it for any other purpose then the land shall revert to me". Is this valid?

The common law disfavors restraints on alienation.
Equity abhors a forfeiture.

A reservation such as I described up there works a forfeiture. Thus it shall be strictly construed against operation. It is not per se void. But it is interpreted strictly against operation - because the common law HATES forfeitures (it also hates restraints on alienation for the same reason: restraints on trade and forfeitures hinder commerce leading to poverty resulting in conflict..
So, the common law disfavors reservations and will interpret them as inapplicable, if possible.

Escrow is a way to avoid scams (French: escroc). Seller has property. Buyer has money. Buyer gives money to escrow holder. Seller gives deed to escrow holder. When escrow holder has those two things, he then gives seller the money and buyer the land. He must however follow their instructions strictly! He is their agent, and thus their fiduciary. Knowledge he has within the scope of his agency, which is limited to the execution of the sales contract, will be conclusively imputed to his principals, i.e. to the buyer and to the seller.

So for example: I give you a deed it says "I, Eric Engle, do renounce and quit claim to any legal interest in Rancha Las Pampas and convey hereby to Tetiana all my legal interest in said property." I give you the deed, However, do not record it.
You enter into the property.
Is your entry rightful? Is it your land?

Your entry is presumptively rightful. The land is presumptively yours, both due to the deed and also due to actual entry i.e. possession. These are legal presumptions, and legal presumptions resolve conflict in cases of doubt! However, a prior recorded deed to the land would in fact oust your interest until you record. Even after you record a quitclaim deed is ONLY me saying "I give up whatever interest in that land i have to you". I can literally give you a quitclaim deed to Alaska! Of course, the true owners will oust you, and the recorder would never record such a deed! But if you enter the land, and hold and develop it, openly notoriously, constantly, for the statutory time (20 years by common law) you acquire legal title by prescription, also known as adverse possession!
A bona fide purchaser for value of a recorded interest in land takes and ousts any other claimant, in principle.

QUESTIONS TO ILLUSTRATE THE RULES
A) I give you a quitclaim deed. I am true owner. My interest was properly recorded. You take the deed I gave you. You do not record. I seek to oust you. What result?
B) I give you a quitclaim deed. I am true owner. My interest was properly recorded. You take the deed I gave you. You do not record. I then give a second deed to your younger sister for the very same land. She records. Whose land is it?
C) I give you a quitclaim deed. I then give your younger sister another quitclaim deed to the very same land. Neither of you record. Whose land is it?

41

ANSWERS

A) The quitclaim grantee has right against the quitclaimer. Recording a deed is prudent and wise and ought be required but is not in fact. The grantee here owns the land.

B) The land is Alice's younger sister's. Alice had the land, but did not record. When Alice's younger sister records she obtains a conclusive presumption to rightful title effectively ousting Alice.

C) "First in time first in right". In a conflict between two unrecorded deeds granted to the same land from the same grantor the earlier in time prevails.

D) I give Alice a warranty deed to land I rightly own in fee simple absolute. I then give Alice's younger sister a quitclaim deed to the same land. Alice's younger sister records her quitclaim deed. Whose land is it?

D) This is an arguable case. The better view, I believe it is also the majority view, regards the land as the warranty grantees, because the warranty deed here guaranties good title, meanwhile the quitclaim deed is only a surrender of a legal interest. I no longer had a legal interest to surrender! The recordation creates a conclusive presumption, but the title was only a quitclaim, not warranted. See, e.g. Fowler v. Will, 19 S. D. 131, 117 Am, St, Eep. 938. ["An unrecorded warranty deed has precedence over a subsequently executed and recorded quitclaim deed purporting to remise, release and quitclaim the grantor's interest in the premises"]

Recordation only protects SUBSEQUENT purchasers in good faith for value

E) I give Tetiana a warranty deed. I then give Alice's younger sister Olha a quitclaim. deed to the same land. Olha records her deed. Olha then sells the land to Christine, by general warranty deed. Christine records. Whose land is it?

E) This too is arguable for the same reason, but the better view is: The land is Christine's. Christine is a good faith purchaser for value with no notice of the cloud on the title. Thus she enjoys the conclusive presumption of good title against all the world

Easements:

An easement is a servitude. A servitude benefits the dominant estate, and burdens the servient estate. A very normal example of an easement is an easements of way, giving the dominant estate the right to pass over the land for ingress or egress. An easement may be express in a written document in which case it is a legal servitude; or it may be imputed by operation of law as an equitable servitude. If the dominant estate is sold the easement is not terminated. If the servient estate is sold the easement is not terminated.

Fee simple:

A fee simple is absolute ownership against all the world save the sovereign. Fees simple may however be subject to conditions subsequent e.g. So they are not necessarily Truly absolute.

Adverse possession:

The wrongful entrant and occupant of land who possess the land openly, notoriously, and in hostile claim of right to the true owner, if not ejected prior to the statutory period, attains title to the land by prescription.

NOTICE IN REAL PROPERTY TRANSACTIONS:

Property in common law is either real or personal
This is just like in the civil law.

In common law we speak of rights as vested, i.e. perfected
when they become immediately enforceable before the court
of law. In contrast, when a right is not immediately enforceable,
but requires some further action before it may be enforced it it
said to be executory. So for example the possession of a wild
animal at common law creates a presumption of ownership.
The property right over the animal vests when the animal is
caught.

"MY *Dear,*

Possession of ferae naturae such as animals,
flowing water, and abandoned property
attaches with caption, i.e. the taking of the animal or thing!"

Say I want to buy land. And you claim to own that land. And you want to sell to me. So you write me out a deed, the easiest being a quitclaim deed. The quitclaim deed says you surrender all your interest in that land to me. I take the deed. I do not record the deed. I have a right to the land, BUT my right might be devested! Meanwhile, you write out another general warranty deed to Olha, and give her the land. Olha records.

Olha is not a good faith purchaser for value! It is a gratuitous transaction, and since she is your sister it might not even be good faith, it could be self-dealing (in sich Geschäft).

BUT

Olha then talks to Christine, and sells Christine the land. Christine gives your sister 10,000 euros. Your sister gives Christine a general warranty deed. Christine, prudent person she is, records the deed.

Now I then say to Christine "NOOOOOOO! MY LAND!" Christine is a subsequent good faith purchaser for value. I did not record. She recorded. So she wins! Christine's recordation of the deed puts the whole world on notice as to who REALLY owns the land. Whether they actually bother to read the deed registry book or not, they know OR SHOULD KNOW that the land is HERS. Constructive means "legal fiction, imputation by operation of law". The presumption of notice is constructive and conclusive in cases of a recorded deed: it is IRREBUTTABLE.

Indexing: the deed must be duly recorded, i.e. properly recorded, to impart constructive notice. Part of recordation is indexing the deed so others can find it. Unindexed=Improperly Recorded=No constructive notice, even though recorded! HOWEVER Indexing has no effect as to the timeliness of recordation. Timestamp, not index number, is the determinant of when the deed is regarded as recorded.

45

CASES
Randall v. Allen - https://casetext.com/case/randall-v-allen
owner of real property executing two conflicting instruments
affecting it, both for a valuable consideration and in favor of an
innocent party, the latter of which instruments in date of execution
is recorded before the former. The statutory rule in such cases is
that the right of the second purchaser for value, whose instrument
is first recorded, is superior, unless the second purchaser had notice
of the existence of the rights of the first purchaser. ... It is not
every kind of possession that is sufficient to constitute or establish
notice. ... The statement that they were living on the property "at
the present time" is immaterial. The critical time is not the present,
but the time when Mrs. Randall took her mortgage. But the
statement that the Allens were "occupying" the property, giving to
that word its usual meaning, and we can hardly presume that it
was used in any other sense in the testimony, would seem to be
sufficient to characterize the possession, particularly when
coupled with the statement as to cultivation. Actual, occupancy
of the land, possessio pedis, has always been held, in the absence
of qualifying circumstances, to be possession of a character
sufficient to constitute or establish notice. ... possession in order
to be sufficient to establish notice must be open, notorious,
 exclusive and visible, and not consistent with the record title. ...
Underlying these requirements is the idea that the circumstances
relied on to establish constructive notice, whether they be
possession or something else, must be such that a prudent man
would be put upon inquiry.

Powell v. Goldsmith
Simple factual summary: escrow holder
does not follow instructions, creating thereby possibility of
recording instruments at times different from those which
were intended by escrow instructions, resulting in fraud.

Simple rule summary:

Knowledge of agent is imputed to principal, even if principal had no actual notice thereof. recording creates a conclusive presumption, but such recordation must be proper. A fraudulent recordation is improper and will not serve constructive notice.

Literal Statements from the case:

"The fact that the knowledge acquired by the agent was not actually communicated to the principal, ... does not prevent operation of the rule .... The agent may have been guilty of a breach of duty to his principal, yet the knowledge has the same effect as to third persons as though his duty had been faithfully performed. The agent acting within the scope of his authority, is, as to the matters existing therein during the course of the agency, the principal himself.

"Notice to an agent in [the] course of a transaction is constructive notice to the principal, and it will not avail the latter to show that the agent failed to communicate to him what he was told. ...This constructive notice, when it exists, is irrebutable. It is not merely prima facie evidence, for then it could be rebutted
"Civil Code section 2898: "A mortgage or deed of trust given for the price of real property, at the time of its conveyance, has priority over all other liens created against the purchaser, subject to the operation of the recording laws."

Simple rule summary:

Knowledge of agent is imputed to principal, even if principal had no actual notice thereof. recording creates a conclusive presumption, but such recordation must be proper. A fraudulent recordation is improper and will not serve constructive notice.

Literal Statements from the case (continued

"where a deed deposited in escrow is fraudulently obtained by the grantee prior to the fulfillment by him of conditions of execution of Note "Civil Code section 1214 provides in part that every conveyance of real property is void as against a subsequent purchaser or mortgagee of the same property in good faith whose conveyance is first recorded. However, Civil Code section 1217 provides that "[a]n unrecorded instrument is valid as between the parties thereto and those who have notice thereof."
"the purpose of Civil Code section 1214 is "to prevent fraud through the withholding of notice of transactions affecting titles, to the detriment of subsequent purchasers in good faith and for valuable consideration, ..." and "... to stimulate and bring about the prompt recordation of all conveyances of real property"
"The priority of a purchase money deed of trust over any liens against a buyer is the primary exception to the general rule that deeds of trust obtain their priority by date of creation or date of recordation. Civil Code section 2898 is intended to protect the seller from the very situation that occurred here, i.e., a third party attempting to insert a lien in ahead of the seller's right to security for the balance of the purchase price.

LYRICAL CASES

Equity Abhors A Forfeiture:

A bank once did sharply contrive
By foreclosure a house to deprive
And how? Listen up! I will sell you your sup'.
Pay attention, 'tis law, logic's shine!
Lender lured her out on a line:
"Don't bankrupt - restructure, it's fine!"
On these words she relied,
and reasonably signed
and then she awaited the loan
But though by these words she was bound,
to honor that loan which she owed,
bank did delay for more than a day

and then moved right on to foreclose.

Foreclosure? A remedy harsh! Disfavored at law! So let's march!
The bank here was prudent 'tis true.
Was lawful as well, is it through?
Nay! Good faith it was not
fair dealing was sought
thus bank at equity have nought!
Unclean hands shall not appear.
For equities balance we here
The debtor, imprudent, went bust!
But lied she did not,
so equity, just,
"regards as done what ought to be done".
Yet,

"Equity follows the law" it is true
The promise? Restructure debt due.
bank can't just foreclose,
but its debt can enforce.
Thus did the court so rule.
Solomonic and wise
the judgement here lies
and justice delights in your eyes.

Take home message: The case which this limerick illustrates shows the complex nature of a real property transaction. The bank holds the legal title to to the land, and then lends money to the possessor of the land, who repay that money. This is commonly called a mortgage (Hypothek). By paying into the mortgage, the court acting in equity may accord protection to the legitimate interests of the borrower. Such remedies however are subject to all the restrictions of equity. As to foreclosure: the bank in this case sought to specifically enforce their contract. Specific performance is an equitable remedy. The court found permitting the bank to dispossess the landowner would be inequitable – **equity abhors a forfeiture**. At the same time, the court in no way reduced the borrowers obligation as a matter of law to repay the money which the lender had lent. Thus this case illustrates the interplay of legal rights and equitable remedies.

PALSGRAF

There once was a very small girl
who wanted to travel the world
she got on a train
and waited in vain
to her home to safely arrive
for found on that train and quite plain
a package of nitro - insane!
Unknown to the rail
unknowable tale
the package i repeat was quite plain...

While hoisting a passenger rough
the package was dropped this is tough
exploded in view
and scales it threw
into the victim so gruff.
The liability here it is plain
a legal duty was found, for the train
contracted with passsangers and traffic was foreseeable
but the inquiry goes further in vain.
Causation in fact there was here
but negligence? Might be unfair
that package, unlabeled, gave no notice "unstable"
So to remedy this damage the court was unable.
Moreover, proximate cause – was it here?
Nay nay! My dear, 'tis quite clear:
even if negligent;
intervening cause, supercedent pause
break the causal chain here.

Held: Not liable. Duty found, but no proximate causation. Even
if proximate no negligence by the railroad for the accident was
unforeseeable due to the negligence of the
passenger in failing to label the package as dangerous..

BOMB BLAST INJURES 13 IN STATION CROWD

Package of Fireworks Explodes in Beach-Bound Throng at East New York.

A PANIC AS TRAIN IS SHAKEN

You Jest at Your Own Risk (Lucy v. Zehmer)

When drinking and jesting of land,
Don't you dare put a pen in your hand!
A document signed,
statute of frauds has defined
suffices to show your intent!
Willfully drunk?
Fully conscious?
You're sunk!
The contract is valid and stands.

Might equity here intercede?
Nay I fear not indeed!
You must come with clean hands
and a drunk understands
he isn't the most moral man.

*Don't Drink
and Deed!*

Avail and cry though he might.
However, the law here was right!
He sold off the land – for cold cash in hand!
So equity let the law stand.

The price might not have been nice,
yet their bargain was struck even twice!!
Undersigned by his wife, so they're screwed for life.
Their intent here quite clear was to sell.

Take home message: You jest at your own peril! The contracting
party in this case sought to go back on their word, and the word
of their spouse, given in writing. Their only tenable argument
would be that they were so drunk as to be unable to form any
intention at all – so called "blind drunk". They were clearly not
so drunk as to lack any conscious perception. The court held them
to their word. Furthermore, there were no equitable reasons for
the court to limit the harsh outcomes of "merely" enforcing legal
rights. So no equitable remedy was found. Presume the court will
hold you – and your clients! - to their own word, one way
(contract, at law) or other (estoppel, in equity).

52

Boston Tea Room - The Case of the Crunchy Chowder!

A diner while chomping on chowder
bit into a bone which crunched louder
She choked on her phlegm,
Then muttered "Ahem!
This is CONTRACTual breach!"

The waiter said "Fine lady no!
Ahoy! We're New England! And so:
IMPLIED WARRANTY? Nay! Nor EXPRESS GUARANTY:
This is our CUSTOM you know!!"

The court listened kindly to both,
The judge then said on their oaths:

"The waiter spoke true. Risk of bone you must chew!
Judgement? Defendant! Now go!

Something is Fishy about this Tale...

In this case an old lady bought chowder, ate it, and choked on a
bone, having to go to the hospital. The rule in such cases is
generally that the eater must be careful of pits in cherries,
stones in beans, and bones in fish, such items which are part of
the food or inherently unavoidable in the production thereof. The
lady argued for an implied warranty, but none was found nor
would be found. In contrast, in cases of impurities introduced
into the food, usually through careless preparation or slipshod
unsanitary practices: where the food is spoiled or has been
contaminated by some foreign substance the court will impose
liability, usually in tort. Plaintiff in such case has a stronger tort
claim than a claim in contract since the contractual damages
would be limited to the cost of the food, strictly speaking.

Enforceable Gratuitous Charitable Promises?

A perpetual promise of prize
Shall never escape from thy eyes
Consideration tis true
Is found here - so sue
at law or in equity wise!

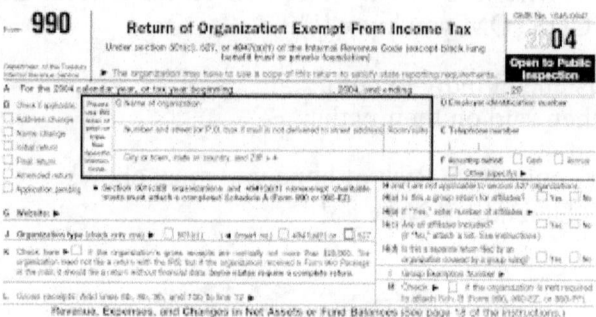

Charitable promises are generally enforced in U.S. common law. The best argument for this result is the fact that the charitable donor obtains good-will for their public pledge. A second best argument is that the promisee has acted in reasonable reliance on the promise, to their detriment. Detrimental reliance claims, brought on a theory of promissory estoppel, only compensate reliance damages, not expectancies such as the benefit of the bargain.

Carbolic Smoke-Ball

Stick my smoke ball up your nose
You won't catch flu and what's more
If I'm wrong I guaranty
A premium fee I'll pay thee!
A Jest? A bet? Nyet!
It was a contract, don't forget!

In this famous case an ad was issued promising to repay the
purchaser of the product if the product did not perform as
desired. The best arguments against enforcement of such
a promise is that it is "mere puffery" or, better, an "offer to
treat", i.e. preliminary negotiation, as opposed to a
"general offer" open to the public. Usually advertisements
are seen as merely an offer to treat, not a general offer
(=offerta ad incertas). In this case however the warranty
was found and upheld, because the product was in fact
purchased due to the inducement of the advertisement.

William v. Walker Thomas Furniture Co.
An Unconscionably Bad Poem!

Electronics I sell may well SHOCK!
But you see my gear is not schlock!
Consumer credit, installment sales,
are the topics of our tale.
So allow me to tell and regale.
"No credit? No problem!" the devise.
At Interest? The law then, device:
Seventeen percent sure ain't cheap!
They take your furniture amd you weep!
Seems like a bit of a creep.

Of bargaining power unequal to mention:
the penalty, late fee, where's your rent then?
CONSCIOUS of social problems yet?
Then don't take this bet!
Doubting THOMAS? No doubt! This "deal"?
WILLIAM! WALK OUT!

This is an example of the idea that an "unsconscionable" contract might not be enforced, namely where its terms are entirely one sided, so that it objectively "shocks the conscience" to enforce such a bargain. These are known as "adhesion" contracts, where there is massively inequal bargaining power and the terms thereof are not negotiable. While this would be readily seen as Wucher in German law, unconscionability has a much weaker legal foundation in U.S. common law due to the lack of a civil code.

Transfer of title:

To transfer title to property, i.e. ownership you must
1) give the property, or a symbol thereof to the donee
2) the donee must accept the donation
Once so done title passes.
There is a rebuttable presumption of acceptance,
since ordinarily property is considered beneficial.
So for example if I give you the key to a house and say "the house
is yours!" I have in principle thereby transferred title to you.

It is yours!

Absent legislation a deed or contract is not required.
However, the statute against frauds might well
require a writing evidencing this transfer.

57

finis